Australian Animals: Through the Looking Glass

**This book is dedicated to my dear grandchildren
- Sydney & Thomas -**

AUSTRALIAN ANIMALS

Through the looking glass

Australian Animals: Through the Looking Glass

First Published in Australia in 2020

ISBN: 978-1-925909-01-2

by Tracy Rockwell
(1955)

Orders: pegasuspublishing@iinet.net.au
www.pegasuspublishing.com.au

PO Box 980, Edgecliff, NSW, 2027

Copyright © Pegasus Publishing
An Ashnong Pty Ltd Company

All rights reserved. No part of this publication may be reproduced, stored in a retrieval system, or transmitted in any form or by any means, electronic, mechanical, photocopying, recording or otherwise, without the prior written permission of the copyright owner. All images used in this publication are in the public domain.

A CIP catalogue record for this book is available from the National Library of Australia.

Other animal books in the series… 'Through the Looking Glass.'

African Animals	Butterflies & Moths
American Animals	Dinosaurs
Asian Animals	European Animals
Australian Animals	Farm Animals
Birds of Australasia	Insects & Bugs
Birds of the World	Sea Creatures

This book takes you on an alphabetical adventure through the animals of Australia. Just roll up a sheet of paper for your telescope, and let's go...

Australia is a big country and continent, with amazing animals, not found anywhere else in the world. Let's take a closer look…

A baby 'Marsupial Mouse'
has a pouch...
for a house!

The 'Blue Tongue Lizard'...
poked, hissed...
and slithered.

You should never ever smile, at a 'Crocodile'!

A great name is Ringo...
for an Australian 'Dingo'!

'Dolphin's' are grey,
and they most love…
to play.

I once knew an 'Echidna', whose name was Belinda!

[An Echidna lays eggs!]

A 'Flying Fox', sleeps rather... unorthodox.

Have you ever considered, a 'Frill Necked Lizard'?

Just a reminder,
to always avoid... a
'Funnel Web Spider'.

[poisonous]

Favourite food for
'Goanna's',
are big yellow bunches of
bonanna's.

Lying in a bog,
is great fun for a 'Frog'.

An Australian 'Kangaroo', just loves to chew!

Do cute little 'Koala's', wear polkadot pyjama's?

Mr. 'Platypus' is amusing...
webbed feet and duck's bill...
but very confusing.

[A Platypus lays eggs!]

Favourite food for a
'Possum', is...
a juicy flower blossom.

This 'Potaroo', is looking at you!

A fun game for a 'Quokka',
is to play beach soccer.

I might look like a doll, but I'm really a 'Spotted Quoll'.

I'm a 'Grey Fur Seal',
who just loves a fish meal.

A big toothy 'Shark',
loves to swim down deep…
in the dark.

A great name for a 'Snake', would be Slippery, Slim or... Jake.

[some are poisonous]

A cute 'Sugar Glider' is a great night rider.

A 'Tasmanian Devil',
can be surprisingly...
very gentle.

A 'Thorny Devil'…
isn't at all easy,
to handle.

Favourite foods for a
'Tree Kangaroo',
are little round berries...
and green bamboo.

What d'ya wanna be?
A walla 'Wallaby'!

The job for a 'Whale',
is to breath, dive deep...
and exhale!

Do you think I'm fat? asked the big brown 'Wombat'.

Australian Animals: Through the Looking Glass

ATTRIBUTIONS

Front Cover - "Eastern Grey Kangaroo with Joey," by John Torcasia (undated). Available at https://www.publicdomainpictures.net/en/view-image.php?image=285710&picture=eastern-grey-kangaroo

Page 9 - "Antichinus" by Sandid (undated). Available at https://www.needpix.com/photo/388176/antechinus-marsupial-mouse-marsupial-native-queensland-australia-wild-pink-nose-pink-ears

Page 11 - "Blotched Blue-tongued Lizard, Austin's Ferry, Tasmania, Australia," by JJ Harrison (2009). Available at https://upload.wikimedia.org/wikipedia/commons/e/e7/Tiliqua_scincoides_scincoides.jpg

Page 13 - "Saltwater crocodile," by fvanrenterghem (2007). Available at https://commons.wikimedia.org/wiki/File:Saltwater_crocodile.jpg

Page 15 - "Dingo at Cleland wildlife park, South Australia," by Peripitus (2008). Available at https://commons.wikimedia.org/wiki/File:Canis_lupus_dingo_-_cleland_wildlife_park.jpg

Page 17 - "Bottle nosed dolphin and babies," by Peter Asprey (2005). Available at https://commons.wikimedia.org/wiki/File:Bottlenose_dolphin_with_young.jpg

Page 19 - "Short-beaked echidna in Australian National Botanic Gardens, Canberra," by Gunjan Pandey (2018). Available at https://upload.wikimedia.org/wikipedia/commons/e/e9/Short-beaked_echidna_in_ANBG.jpg

Page 21 - "Grey headed flying fox preparing to take off. Photo taken in Roma Street Parklands, Brisbane, QLD," by Andrew Mercer (2019). Available at https://commons.wikimedia.org/wiki/File:Grey_headed_flying_fox_-_taking_off_-_AndrewMercer_IMG41558.jpg

Page 23 - "Frill Necked Lizard, Kakadu, NT," by Matt (2013). Available at https://upload.wikimedia.org/wikipedia/commons/f/f1/Frill-necked_Lizard_%28Chlamydosaurus_kingii%29_%288692622586%29.jpg

Page 25 - "A female funnel web spider," by David McClenaghan, (CSIRO), (2002). Available at https://commons.wikimedia.org/wiki/File:CSIRO_ScienceImage_2226_A_Female_Funnel_Web_Spider.jpg

Page 27 - "Common goanna, Featherdale Wildlife Park, Sydney," by Sardaka (2017). Available at https://upload.wikimedia.org/wikipedia/commons/5/5/%281%29Goanna-5.jpg

Page 29 - "White-lipped green tree frog," by Bignoter (2017). Available at https://commons.wikimedia.org/wiki/File:Green_Tree_Frog_0277.jpg

Page 31 - "Macropus rufus, female in conservation reserve, Blue Mountains, Australia," by Lilly M (2008). Available at https://commons.wikimedia.org/wiki/File:Kangaroo_Australia_01_11_2008_-_retouch.jpg

Page 33 - "Koala, Bonorong Wildlife Park, Tasmania, Australia," by JJ Harrison (2010). Available at https://en.wikipedia.org/wiki/Koala#/media/File:Phascolarctos_cinereus_Bonorong.jpg

Page 35 - "Platypus in mountain stream," by Maria Grist (2018). Available at https://commons.wikimedia.org/wiki/File:Platypus_swimming.jpg

Page 37 - "Common Brushtail Possum, Austin's Ferry, Tasmania, Australia," by JJ Harrison - (2009). Available at https://commons.wikimedia.org/wiki/File:Trichosurus_vulpecula_1.jpg

Page 39 - "Tasmanian Bettong, Waterworks Reserve, Tasmania, Australia," by JJ Harrison (2010). Available at https://commons.wikimedia.org/wiki/File:Bettongia_gaimardi.jpg

Page 41 - "Quokka adult and child on Rottnest Island" by Pchampin (2017). Available at https://commons.wikimedia.org/wiki/File:Quokka.jpeg

Page 43 - "Tiger Quoll," by Michael J Fromholtz (2011). Available at https://commons.wikimedia.org/wiki/File:Spotted_Tail_Quoll_2011.jpg

Page 45 - "Australian Fur Seal," by Bernard Spragg. NZ (2014). Available at https://commons.wikimedia.org/wiki/File:New_Zealand_Fur_seal._FZ200_(14502352505).jpg

Page 47 - "Great white shark," by Hermanus Backpackers (2009). Available at https://commons.wikimedia.org/wiki/File:Great_white_shark_south_africa.jpg

Page 49 - "Tiger Snake," by Catching The Eye (2012). Available at https://www.flickr.com/photos/160417453@N04/27079559468

Page 51 - "Sugar Glider," by andyround62 (2016). Available at https://pixabay.com/photos/australian-wildlife-sugar-glider-1675479/

Page 53 - "Tasmanian devil," by Keres H (2007). Available at https://commons.wikimedia.org/wiki/File:Tasmanian_devil_head_on.jpg

Page 55 - "A Thorny Devil Stands Steadfast beside the road," by M.c.e.1999 (2016). Available at https://commons.wikimedia.org/wiki/File:Thorny_Devil_(Coolgardie).jpg

Page 57 - "Goodfellows Tree Kangaroo" by David Lochlin (2014). Available at https://www.flickr.com/photos/dlochlin/14363963136

Page 59 - "Swamp Wallaby at Lone Pine Koala Sanctuary, Brisbane, Australia," by Quartl (2009). Available at https://commons.wikimedia.org/wiki/File:Red-Necked_Wallaby_Front.jpg

Page 61 - "Underwater photograph of humpback whales," by Christopher Michael (2014). Available at https://commons.wikimedia.org/wiki/File:Humpback_Whales_-_South_Bank.jpg

Page 63 - "Wombat" by Chris Fithall (2019). Available at https://www.flickr.com/photos/chrisfithall/47676382231.

THE END

Other animal books in the series...
'Through The Looking Glass.'

African Animals
American Animals
Asian Animals
Australian Animals
Birds of Australasia
Birds of the World

Butterflies & Moths
Dinosaurs
European Animals
Farm Animals
Insects & Bugs
Sea Creatures

www.ingramcontent.com/pod-product-compliance
Lightning Source LLC
Chambersburg PA
CBHW051248110526
44588CB00025B/2916